THINK RIVER, NOT PIE

THINK RIVER, NOT PIE

LIFE LESSONS DESIGNED TO INSPIRE
EXTRAORDINARY LIVING

KIRK BOWMAN

XULON ELITE

Xulon Press Elite
2301 Lucien Way #415
Maitland, FL 32751
407.339.4217
www.xulonpress.com

Exulon Elite

© 2023 by Kirk Bowman

All rights reserved solely by the author. The author guarantees all contents are original and do not infringe upon the legal rights of any other person or work. No part of this book may be reproduced in any form without the permission of the author.

Due to the changing nature of the Internet, if there are any web addresses, links, or URLs included in this manuscript, these may have been altered and may no longer be accessible. The views and opinions shared in this book belong solely to the author and do not necessarily reflect those of the publisher. The publisher therefore disclaims responsibility for the views or opinions expressed within the work.

Unless otherwise indicated, Scripture quotations taken from the New American Standard Bible (NASB). Copyright © 1960, 1962, 1963, 1968, 1971, 1972, 1973, 1975, 1977, 1995 by The Lockman Foundation. Used by permission. All rights reserved.

Paperback ISBN-13: 978-1-6628-7961-6
Ebook ISBN-13: 978-1-6628-7962-3

Table of Contents

1 2
Never let anyone but God define your life.
You are the one who has to live with your choices.

2 4
You can be right or you can have relationships.

3 6
Don't drag rocks around your whole life.

4 8
Live on a full tank.

5 10
Worship is a gift from God.
It reorients everything to the ultimate reality of the greatness of God.

6 12
You can't pull on the leaves and make the tree grow.

7 14
Think river, not pie.

8 16
Don't make a big decision in the middle of a storm.
You'll regret it on a sunny day.

9 18
Walk away from wells of contention & enmity and dig another well.

10. 20
Your value as a human being is never found in comparison to others but always found in your uniqueness.

11. 22
People get on & off the bus in life and in church.

12. 24
You can't live a great life alone.
So better learn to get along with and work with people.

13. 26
Your presence matters more than you think it does.
Always give the gift of your presence to the people you love the most.

14. 28
If you will build God's house, God will build your house.
Guess who wins on that deal?

15. 30
Your marriage is the center of a great family.
Your kids will want to be the center of attention.
Don't let them. For everyone's good.

16. 32
Your life is not happening to you but through you.

17. 34
Burn the oil, not the wick.

18. 36
Don't judge my work with your theories.

19. 38
If God can get it through you, God will get it to you.

20. 40
Forgiveness doesn't mean letting hurtful people remain in your life to continue to hurt you.

21 .... **42**
Life will schedule enough pain for you, so you might as well schedule your pleasure.

22 .... **44**
It's almost always a green light until you get a red light.

23 .... **46**
If you want God's hand on your life, find out where His hand is—and get under it.

24 .... **48**
You find what you're looking for, so make sure you look for the right things.

25 .... **50**
Loyalty is tested by adversity.

26 .... **52**
Tithing really does open the windows of Heaven.
90 percent blessed is always better than 100 percent cursed.

27 .... **54**
Be nice to yourself.

28 .... **56**
God is a God of abundance.
Life is full of abundance.
There is no shortage.

29 .... **58**
God so loved the world, He did not send a committee.

30 .... **60**
Your life grows by giving, not by taking.

31 .... **62**
You're hungry for what you have been eating and thirsty for what you have been drinking.

32 .... **64**
Excellence may cost more.
But it's always worth it.

33 .... **66**
You will become just like the people you hang around with.

34 .... **68**
Love is the perfect bond of unity.

35 .... **70**
God loves you just like you are! But He also loves you enough to not leave you that way.

36 .... **72**
Let the game come to you.

37 .... **74**
If you'll change your mind, you can change your life.

38 .... **76**
A word from God, in your heart and in your mouth, will direct your life.

39 .... **78**
Keep walking through your valley of despair.

40 .... **80**
Smoking won't send you to Hell.
It just makes you smell like you've been there.

41 .... **82**
I'd rather die believing than live doubting.

42 .... **84**
The answer is always no if you don't ask.

43 .... **86**
The seeds you sow in private bear their fruit in public.

44 88
The most important person in your life is You.

45 90
An estimate is the lie you tell yourself to get started on a project.

46 92
Goals are great because of the person you have to become to achieve them.

47 94
God is always, eventually faithful.

48 96
Lack of communication is the breeding ground for vain imaginations.

49 98
The God who created everything, owns everything, & controls everything is FOR you.

50 100
Build in the valley what God has shown you on the mountain.

51 102
"Sorry" won't win the battle.

52 104
You are not the star of the show.

53 106
The right direction is more important than perfection.

54 108
You hear the signals you are tuned in to.

55 110
Stay in your lane.
There is an ease and a grace for you there.

56 112
You can run your life from your prayer closet.

57 114
Sometimes, the best call is to defer.

58 116
It all started in a garden.

59 118
When you move, God moves.
So, make a move and give Him something to bless.

60 120
Pray the promise, not the problem.

61 122
There is a battle at the gate of every new season or level of life.

62 124
Many decisions are made emotionally, and then a rationale is built afterward to justify that decision.

63 126
Planted people prosper.

64 128
We don't see the world as it is. We see the world as we are.

65 130
Face the facts and declare the truth.

66 132
Wherever you go, there you are.

Foreword:

This book began as a fun little project. On the occasion of my sixty-sixth birthday, I decided to post sixty-six life lessons on my Facebook page. All throughout these postings, so many were urging me to put my life lessons in a book. So, here it is.

I pray these lessons will be as helpful to you as they have been to me.

Much love to you all! God is for you!

1

Never let anyone but God define your life.

You are the one who has to live with your choices.

In my early years of ministry, I used to let people's opinions about what kind of car I drove or what kind of house I lived in really affect me. I realized I was left driving the car that pleased someone, and they left the church or my life, and they were gone now, and I was stuck with that car.

Other people's opinions do not pay your bills.

So, as long as I feel like I am pleasing God with my choices, that's all that really matters.

2

You can be right or you can have relationships.

I have very few regrets in life but not knowing this truth earlier on is one of my few regrets. I lost a lot of good relationships along the way insisting on being right rather than valuing the relationship.

I realize there are certain places we have to take a strong stand on, but there are lots of places we can choose grace, mercy, and deference in our relationships.

Kudos to my longsuffering bride for putting up with me all the years I was learning this lesson.

3

Don't drag rocks around your whole life.

You can't do anything with the unwilling, so quit trying. You can only work with the willing.

Trying to work with the unwilling is like dragging rocks. When you stop pulling, they stop moving. It's exhausting to you and aggravating to them.

Find people with a fire in their belly and feed that fire.

4

Live on a full tank.

I had a friend growing up who only put the minimal amount of gas in his car. Just enough to not run out. I suggested to him, "Let's fill the car up once and then just put gas in as it goes down a little. That way, we are not always living on the edge of disaster."

Better to live off of a full tank then off of the fumes of an empty tank. Stay full and create margin in your life.

Whether it's your finances, your emotional health, your spiritual health, or your relationships. Keep those tanks full. Give yourself some margin to breathe.

There is precious treasure and oil in the dwelling of the wise, But a foolish man swallows it up. (Proverbs 21:20)

5

Worship is a gift from God.

It reorients everything to the ultimate reality of the greatness of God.

The ultimate, lasting reality is that God is good. And He loves us immensely!

Circumstances, seasons, people, my feelings, and troubles come and go. They are things that come to pass.

What always lasts and is always true is the greatness and goodness of God.

Whether I feel good or not, God is still good and is always worthy of worship!

So, worship is actually a gift to keep me tethered to the greatest reality there is—God's greatness and goodness.

6

You can't pull on the leaves and make the tree grow.

We live in a fast food, overnight delivery, Amazon Prime, fast paced world now. We want it now! Or at least by tomorrow.

Let's remember it all started in a garden. The things that really matter in life grow at an agricultural pace rather than a technological pace.

Growing your finances; building your church or business; true, lasting relationships; developing wisdom and solid character; finding your own voice; they all take time to grow.

Whatever you're trying to grow, give it some time— some love, some attention, some intention. Don't be lazy about it, but don't try to rush the growth of the tree.

7

Think river, not pie.

This lesson has literally been a life changer for me!

The Bible says there is a river flowing from the throne of God. Whenever I see a waterfall, I think of the idea that water has been flowing for years and will continue to flow for many years. Abundance just keeps flowing!

When we have a "pie mentality" toward life, we hold on tightly to our pieces of the pie because we think it's all we have. When we have a "river mentality," we know more is coming if we keep letting it flow through us.

So don't stop the flow and get constipated!

There is no shortage of money, opportunity, blessing, or favor. The big secret is, don't restrict yourself with a pie mentality. Set yourself free with a river mentality!

8

Don't make a big decision in the middle of a storm.

You'll regret it on a sunny day.

Life is full of storms. No one, no matter who they are, escapes the storms of life. Winds blow. Rain falls. On everyone.

Life is also full of sunny days. I can see clearly now, the rain is gone.

When storms are around us, it can feel like they are going to last forever. But storms come to pass. They run out of rain.

So, don't quit the job, the ministry, the relationship, the plan, or the goal. Don't quit on yourself in the middle of the storm.

Sunny days are up ahead.

9

Walk away from wells of contention & enmity and dig another well.

In Genesis 26, Isaac prospered in the days of famine because he continued to sow seed and dig wells.

Some of those wells were fought over, and Isaac recognized and named them "contention" and "enmity." Isaac walked away from those wells and kept digging wells until he finally reached his Rehoboth well—a place of wide-open space.

All of us will face contentions; enmity, betrayals, unfair situations, bad deals, and misunderstandings.

You can't spend your whole life fighting over wells of contention. Or enmity. It can swallow all your time, thoughts, and energy. Some battles are not worth the blood they shed.

Turn the other cheek. Walk away. And dig another well.

10

Your value as a human being is never found in comparison to others but always found in your uniqueness.

Comparison is so easy to do today. With social media so prevalent, it's easy to compare their "highlight reel" with your everyday life.

How big their church is, the vacations they take—and how often—the friends they have, the house they live in, and on and on and on.

One of the 10 commandments is "Do not covet." Don't want what others have. Enjoy what you have.

God didn't have one of you, so that's why He made you. He wanted one of you. Your style, your personality, your giftings, your sense of humor, your perspective.

God wants you to be you. We want you to be you!

No one wins in the comparison game. We either feel inferior or superior. Neither one of those are good.

It's been said, and it's true, comparison is the thief of joy!

11

People get on & off the bus in life and in church.

In my earlier years of ministry, I struggled mightily with people leaving; our church, my life. It really hurt me and bothered me a lot. Quite painful, really.

The bus analogy has helped me a lot.

People get on. People get off. But the bus is still going toward the place God wants it to go. The vision doesn't change because of people getting off.

Some people are just on for a season. It's ok to let them gracefully get off the bus when their time is done.

Those who can leave you, let them go. If someone can leave, wants to leave, let them go. Their season with you is up.

God always has new people to help create the new season

There will always be some who stick with you through it all. What a treasure they are.

12

You can't live a great life alone.

So better learn to get along with and work with people.

A great life is always a team sport.

Whether it is church, family, or business. No one has all the gifts and perspectives needed to build something great. We all need other people in our life.

I've known so many people who were so smart, so talented, and so gifted. But they couldn't get along with other people. They always ended up struggling.

Always finding fault with people, their boss, their coworkers, their church, where they work. We all know—if you're looking for faults, you'll always find them because no one or nothing is perfect.

Your best life will always be full of great partnerships.

So, learn to get along with others.

13

Your presence matters more
than you think it does.

Always give the gift of your
presence to the people
you love the most.

When our daughter, Elizabeth, was in high school, she played soccer for her school team. Suzette and I showed up for just about every game. Girls' high school soccer is not all that compelling to watch. But no matter what the weather, we showed up.

Several years ago, In one of the worst seasons of pastoring our church, we were completely downcast. We got away for a few days to try and breathe a little. Two of our best friends showed up on their initiative. They didn't give us advice or counsel. They just showed up and told us they loved us and believed in us.

It's Impossible to show up for everything for everybody. But when you do show up, giving the gift of your presence, it matters a lot.

So, whether it's a celebration or a difficulty, the power of your presence makes a huge difference.

Presence matters more than words of advice.

14

If you will build God's house, God will build your house.

Guess who wins on that deal?

Old Testament King David wanted to build a house for God. God told him, "Because you desire to build My House, I'm going to build your House."

Church—God's House—is God's idea!

The House of God is the gate of Heaven. God walks into the world through His Church. People walk into God through His Church.

Jesus loves His Church so much, He laid down His life for her. Jesus is building His Church, and I want to build with Him.

There is no perfect church. If you found one, you shouldn't go—because then it wouldn't be perfect anymore.

Church is messy. People get hurt in church. But in all her imperfections, God still loves His Church. God still uses His Church. God is still building His Church.

I have been a believer and a Church builder for almost fifty years! My real-life testimony is: God will build my house when I give my best to build His House.

15

Your marriage is the center of a great family.

Your kids will want to be the center of attention.

Don't let them. For everyone's good.

The most important human relationship you have in life is your marriage partner. It's a different relationship from any other relationship.

It's part of your development as a person to stay committed to someone for a whole lifetime. To keep adjusting to make your marriage work. To keep it fun. To make it meaningful. To keep it loving. To keep it sweet.

Kids, by their very nature, will suck all the air out of the room.

When they are small, they take a lot of attention. When they are teenagers, they can get pretty funky attitudes.

When they move out on their own, they will always remain your kids, and you will still be concerned for their well-being.

It is our job to love our kids unconditionally, but our relationship with our kids is always on the perimeter of our family.

Kids feel more secure when their mom & dad's relationship is strong—and at the center of the family.

Husband and wife at the center of a family is a healthy move for the whole family.

16

Your life is not happening to you but through you.

Watch over your heart, your inner man, with all diligence, for from it flows the issues of life.

One translation says, "From your heart flow the borders of your life."

This has been one of the most profound and pivotal life lessons I have ever learned.

It's not what happens to you that matters so much; it's what is happening in you that matters most.

When we choose to fill our hearts with peace, love, prosperity, blessing, favor, joy, and kindness, that's what our lives become.

When we allow bitterness, unforgiveness, anger, resentment, self-pity, and poverty to fill our hearts, then that's what our lives become.

Watching over my heart with diligence means I really have to pay attention, on a continual basis, to what's really going inside me.

17

Burn the oil, not the wick.

The wick of an oil lamp draws up the oil and doesn't burn down itself.

You may be gifted, intelligent, and talented, but that will only carry you so far. You can't depend on your own gifts and talents. You have to depend on the oil, the Holy Spirit's anointing, flowing through you.

The price for oil is TIME; Time spent with God—in His Word, in prayer, in His presence.

Jesus told Martha that she was worried about so many things, but Mary had chosen the ONE NECESSARY THING: sitting at Jesus's feet.

Arrange your life so that you always give time to the One Necessary Thing! Spend that time with Jesus and buy up the oil!

18

*Don't judge my work
with your theories.*

It's always amazing to me how people will be so full of opinions on what our church or what I, as a pastor, ought to be doing.

I am a cheerleader to anyone who is putting in the work to build anything—church, business or ministry—because I know the reality of how hard the work can be.

The people who are actually doing the work will often have a whole different perspective than those just judging from the sidelines.

Constructive criticism is best given by those who have actually constructed something.

I definitely want input from those who have actually built something. But I am not really interested in unproven theories from those who aren't really in the game.

19

If God can get it through you, God will get it to you.

God always intends to bless us to make us a blessing.

The blessing is never intended to stop at us but to flow through us.

So, God gives us peace to minister peace, joy to minister joy, grace to minister grace, and love to minister love.

The two aspects of this concept are important. We have to get it to give it. We then have to give it to get more.

It's hard to minister peace when you are all stressed out or to minister joy when you are bummed out.

This principle applies to our finances so well. God supplies seeds to sowers and then increases harvest to us.

If we get constipated, the flow stops! If we keep the flow going – God knows who to get it to—those who keep the flow going.

20

Forgiveness doesn't mean letting hurtful people remain in your life to continue to hurt you.

It took me a few years to realize this truth.

The real value in forgiving others is setting your own soul free from them.

We can't let others live rent free in our heads and hearts. The pain they caused in the past doesn't have to stay with us in an ongoing way.

But forgiveness and trust are two separate categories. Trust is a necessary ingredient in any relationship.

Even Jesus said He didn't trust Himself into the hands of everyone.

Some people are toxic and mean. It's hard to realize that when you are not that way.

We need to forgive for our own soul's sake. We need boundaries from toxic people as well.

21

Life will schedule enough pain for you, so you might as well schedule your pleasure.

No one, no matter how nice or smart or holy, escapes pain in life. It's just a part of life on this fallen planet.

So, schedule in your celebrations in life. Celebrate your birthday. Your anniversary. Special occasions. Put it on the calendar!

In the Old Testament, feasts (parties) were locked into the schedule of the Israelites. God wanted Israel to remember and celebrate.

Jesus's first miracle was to keep a party going. He changed water into wine so the party would be kept going.

Your soul needs times to press pause, remember, celebrate, and enjoy. It's part of your wholeness in life!

22

It's almost always a green light until you get a red light.

Sometimes, people are waiting for God to tell them what to do rather than just making an educated, Godly decision and moving forward with it.

There are important factors involved in making a good decision—Godly counsel from trusted sources, making sure we are Biblically aligned, playing the movie through on where the decision might take you, and so on.

Instead of waiting for a green light to appear, realize you have a green light already and that God knows how to give you a red light on that decision. If He wants to stop you, He knows how to let you know that.

It's easier to steer a moving bike than a stationary one.

23

If you want God's hand on your life, find out where His hand is—and get under it.

Instead of asking God to bless what you want to do, start seeking out what He is doing and begin to cooperate with that.

God's hand is always on His Church—so get involved in that.

God's hand is on Godly relationships—so quit trying to get God's blessing on that relationship that isn't honoring to Him.

There are certain things God is doing in certain seasons. When you see those things, start moving toward them.

Find out what God is doing. Find out where God is blessing, and get under that rather than always asking God to bless what you are doing.

24

You find what you're looking for, so make sure you look for the right things.

If we are in a room and I ask you to look for brown things or blue things, you will find what you are looking for just because you started looking for them.

If you start looking for what's wrong in a situation (or a person), you will find it. If you start looking for what's right in a situation (or a person), you will find that as well.

We all possess a reticular activating system. Your brain will notice and start picking up on what you have decided to notice.

So, make sure you are looking for reasons and not excuses; positives and not negatives. Things to be grateful for rather than what's wrong. The upside and not the downside. The way forward rather than why things can't go forward. Reasons to believe rather than reasons to doubt.

You'll never live a positive life with a negative mindset.

25

Loyalty is tested by adversity.

When things are going well for you, a lot of people just hang around because they like the overflow of what happens to them. They like what's happening for them while things go well for you.

You'll discover your true friends and those who really love you when you walk through a season of adversity.

This is one reason I encourage couples to go through a summer and winter together before they get serious with each other. Lasting love is not just infatuated with the glow of summer. Lasting love loves the person, not just what they can do for you.

In a season of adversity, you'll discover who are the fair-weather friends, the predators, and the true friends.

Seasons of adversity aren't really fun, but they definitely reveal things—and people.

26

Tithing really does open the windows of Heaven.

90 percent blessed is always better than 100 percent cursed.

Suzette and I have paid tithe for decades. I'm so glad my first pastor taught me to honor God with tithe.

Our primary motivation in paying tithe is to honor God with our first and best. He deserves more than our left overs.

Incredibly, God promises to pour out blessing on our lives if we honor Him with our first and best. He could just require us to pay tithe, but He actually promises a reward.

The tithe breaks the power of the curse and releases the power of God's blessing.

Life is hard enough blessed. Why make it harder than it needs to be? Pay your tithe and honor God!

27

Be nice to yourself.

I play golf. It's a love/hate relationship.

Golf is exceedingly difficult, and yet, when I am playing, well, it is amazingly delightful.

Often, when I hit a bad shot, I will talk to myself more negatively than I would ever talk to anyone else.

I think a lot of us are much harder on ourselves than we need to be. Negative self-talk can dominate our mind way more often than it should.

You're not perfect. I'm not perfect. But I think we're doing better than we give ourselves credit for.

If you're going to love your neighbor as you love yourself, you ought to at least like yourself. A little.

God is exceedingly in love with you. So, it really is ok to be nice to yourself. Really!

28

God is a God of abundance.

Life is full of abundance.

There is no shortage.

One of the revelations that has had a huge impact on my life and thinking is to adopt an "abundance mentality."

An abundance mentality helps us realize there is more than enough resource for everything we need in life. There's lots of money, talent, and help available. The issue is how to get it to flow to us.

It's all flowing somewhere. Might as well get it to flow to and through us.

A "scarcity mentality" will shrink your world. You will hold on to and hoard what you have. It will make your world smaller and smaller.

Abundance recognizes no one else's success ever takes anything away from me. I can rejoice at their success because there is enough success to go around for everyone.

Abundance-thinking fuels a spirit of generosity. I can freely give because I know there is so much more coming.

If you want to have a free spirit, abundance-thinking is a big part of it.

29

God so loved the world, He did not send a committee.

God always raises up leaders to do His will on the earth.

The Bible is full of stories of leaders: Moses, Abraham, David, Paul, Peter, Jesus—all leaders called by God to lead the way in whatever God's call was on their lives, all called to lead the way in what God wants done on the earth.

Committees may help manage things somewhat safely, but "committee-thinking" will never bring real breakthrough.

Leadership is more about responsibility than privilege. A leader feels the responsibility to make sure the vision comes to pass.

I believe every one of us has some kind of leadership calling on our life—something God wants us to feel a sense of responsibility for to make sure a project or idea comes to fruition.

30

Your life grows by giving, not by taking.

The law of sowing and reaping is the operational law of all of life.

Life gives back what and how you give out.

So, if you want tomatoes, plant tomato seeds. If you want corn, plant corn seeds. If you want a lot of corn, plant a lot of corn seeds.

It's easy to get obsessed with what we are getting out of life. But over time, what really matters will be what we are giving.

If you want mercy, sow mercy.

If you want love, sow love.

If you want money, sow money.

If you want friends, sow friendliness.

It is an amazing concept to consider that we have the power to create our future by what we sow today.

31

You're hungry for what you have been eating and thirsty for what you have been drinking.

When I first met Suzette, she was quite into eating and drinking in a healthy way. My upbringing never included that way of thinking.

From her influence, I started drinking lots of water and stopped drinking soft drinks. After a couple of months of just drinking water, I took a sip of a soft drink. It tasted awful to me.

I've found the more I pray, the more I want to pray. The more I read my Bible, the more I worship, the more I eat healthy, the more I exercise, the more I want of those things.

Making those positive changes is a little hard at first. But then, the momentum starts to work in your favor.

Blessed are those who hunger and thirst for righteousness, for they will be filled.

32

Excellence may cost more.

But it's always worth it.

God is a God of excellence. We represent Him well when we aim for excellence in our lives, ministries, families, or business.

To offer halfhearted attempts in serving God undersells God and ourselves.

Daniel represented God well during Israel's Babylonian captivity. The Bible says he was ten times better than all the secular leaders. He represented God with excellence in a culture that did not really honor God.

Excellence is:
Doing our best
Giving our best
Being our best
For the Glory of God.

Sometimes, we have to chew on mediocrity on our way to excellence.

Sometimes, excellence feels like it may cost too much.

But once you've stepped up to excellence in all arenas of your life, you'll be glad you did.

33

You will become just like the people you hang around with.

One of the most important, life impacting lessons is this one: You will become just like the people you hang around with.

If you hang around positive, faith-filled, loving, God-loving people, your life will trend that way. If you hang around negative, cynical, fault-finding, excuse-finding people, your life will trend that way.

The Bible says, "Bad company corrupts good morals." (1 Cor. 15:33).

If you have on white gloves and started digging around in the dirt with them, your gloves get dirty. Your dirt does not get "glovey."

Peer pressure is not just an issue for a teenager. Everyone is impacted by peer pressure.

Choose your circle of friends wisely. They are literally shaping you and your future.

34

Love is the perfect bond of unity.

When Suzette and I first began building our church, our hearts were full of vision for the church we wanted to build.

We went to work with a pretty clear picture of the kind of church we were called to build. We declared that vision and worked hard to build it.

For years, we sought to gather people around the vision of the house, even to unify people around that vision.

As the many seasons of life have come and gone, I have come to realize that love is the perfect bond of unity— not vision.

Even if the vision is super clear to me, it will still be seen differently by others. That's the human condition.

A clear vision is important, but love is what will actually keep us connected.

Love keeps families connected. Friendships connected. Churches connected. Movements connected.

Love is the super glue of unity.

35

God loves you just like you are!
But He also loves you enough
to not leave you that way.

It's a wonderful revelation to know that God is completely in love with us.

There's nothing we could do to make Him love us more. There's nothing we could do make Him love us less.

The One who knows us best. The One who knows the most. Is the One who loves us the best—and the most.

Within that certainty of love, God is still working on us to help us become better.

Attitudes, personality quirks, funky thought patterns, family of origin issues, besetting sins, self-defeating behavior.

We all have stuff that could shipwreck us.

Thank God, He is always working to help us grow out of these things and into all we can be.

36

Let the game come to you.

In my early years of leadership and ministry, I tried too hard, thinking too much depended on me.

I often found myself striving and grinding, trying to make things happen.

I was like a person carrying the canoe rather than just getting in it and letting it carry me along.

God has apportioned to each one of us a measure of grace. That measure has some limitations to it. Some boundaries. But it also has some divine empowerment in it.

Each one of us has a grace lane. Live in that grace lane and let the game come to you.

37

If you'll change your mind, you can change your life.

There is incredible power in our mindsets.

We can be transformed by the renewing of our minds.

When we accept Christ, we are made right and given a position of righteousness.

Now, we spend the rest of our lives adjusting our thinking:
- Paradigms
- Outlook
- Behavior
- Approach
- Style

To fit what we have become in Christ.

We can:
Transform
Renew
Get an upgrade
On any area of our life if we'll change our mind about it.

We can:
Improve our relationships
Have a fun & loving family
Succeed at work
Increase our finances
Get better & better at ministry
Upgrade our walk with God

The beauty of being a human being created in the image of God is we can change—our minds and our lives.

You can change—starting today.

38

A word from God, in your heart and in your mouth, will direct your life.

God's Word is full of life and energy. It contains the power to fulfill itself. God even watches over His Word to perform it.

When the Holy Spirit speaks a "Now Word" out of God's eternal Word to us, we can take that promise and fill our hearts and our mouths with it.

What really lives in your heart is so important. It is a matter of life or death.

The words we speak are so powerful. They create things. They move things. They guide our lives.

The Bible says our tongue—our words—are like a rudder to a ship. It doesn't matter which way the winds are blowing; it's the set of the rudder that ultimately guides the ship.

When you wake up at 3 a.m. and your thoughts start to go negative, speak God's Word—to yourself and to your situation.

When you are faced with negative news at 3 p.m. in the afternoon, locate a promise from God's Word. Fill your heart with it. Keep it in your mouth.

And direct your life.

39

Keep walking through your valley of despair.

If you will keep walking through your valleys of despair and learn your lessons there, you'll always come out brighter on the other side.

Around fifteen or twenty years ago, our church went through a difficult and horrible season. There were some pretty severe issues going on with our staff that literally almost caused our church to unravel.

It seemed like it would never end. But, eventually it did.

I can remember so well the despair I felt as this season just seemed like it was completely out of my control.

All I knew to do was keep moving forward. One step at a time.

Since then, thousands of people have been reached for Jesus. Dozens of mission trips have taken place. Multiple thousands of lives have been touched and changed for the good.

I've seen lots of people quit in the valley. Who knows what their story may have been if they just kept putting one step in front of the other?

If you're going through a valley season, keep moving forward. God is faithful, and you will come out better on the other side.

40

Smoking won't send you to Hell.

It just makes you smell
like you've been there.

When I first gave my life to Christ as an eighteen-year-old young man, I had a lot of adjustments to make in my lifestyle. I spent my teenage years getting high on something just about every day.

For some reason, stopping all the substance abuse was pretty much immediate. But to stop smoking cigarettes took some time for me.

My first few years as a Christian were focused on getting rid of the garbage in my life. I was focused on behavior changes.

Behavior change is important, but Jesus didn't just come to make us behave; He came to give us an abundant life.

Abundant life is more about believing than behaving.

Good believing turns into good behaving at some point, but the more important issue that needs change is what we really believe.

So yeah, it's probably a good idea to stop smoking. Not really good for you. But way more important is to work on our BS (belief systems).

That's where true living comes from.

41

I'd rather die believing than live doubting.

There are a couple of people that have become heroes of mine. Their names are not famous. Some of them did not accomplish a lot in the world's eyes.

But they believed God for His touch on their life till their very last breath. They trusted God until their last moment on the planet.

We all get to choose how to live:

Full of faith or full of doubt
Worshipping or complaining
Positive or negative
Grateful or cynical

I hope to carry a spirit of faith until my very last breath on this planet. Trusting God. Hopeful. Grateful. Worshipping.

Doubting is easy. Cynical is easy. Negative is easy. Fault finding is easy. It takes some strength and character to choose faith, hope, and love until the very end.

I want to be found faithful, carrying the faith on my watch all the way through to the finish line.

42

The answer is always no if you don't ask.

Jesus said we should ask and keep asking, seek and keep seeking, and knock and keep knocking.

It's a posture of movement and expectation for us to take in life.

No one ever knows it all. There are new discoveries, new opportunities, new rooms to walk in to.

The answer is always no if we don't ask.

The solution is always hidden if we don't seek.

The door is always closed if we don't knock.

I always, politely, ask if there is a possibility for an upgrade. On the flight. At the hotel. Sometimes, the answer is no, but sometimes, the answer is yes.

I always ask if people want to receive Jesus at the end of every message I teach, no matter the subject I just taught on, and someone usually says yes.

Don't count yourself out before you even give yourself the opportunity. Don't assume the door is closed before you even knock on it. Don't trap yourself in a problem if you haven't even sought a solution.

Keep asking, seeking, and knocking.

43

The seeds you sow in private bear their fruit in public.

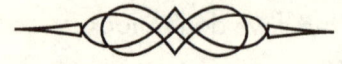

I have an on again, off again relationship with exercise.

In one of my on seasons, I was travelling somewhere and at a hotel. One morning, I got up early and was on the treadmill. No one else was in the room.

It occurred to me, no one will ever know I was up early and exercising. No one would see me exercising, but everyone would be able to see the results of my exercise later.

I think most of the seeds that create a great life are sown when no one else is watching.

Reading my Bible. Worshipping God early in the morning. Having my prayer time. Exercising. What I watch on TV or online. What I don't watch. Saving money or spending it all. What I eat or don't eat.

All of these things are sowing seeds in private places. No one sees those decisions and actions taking place.

But eventually, the seed sown in private places bears its fruit in public places.

44

The most important person in your life is You.

When you get on a plane, they tell you, "In case of an emergency, oxygen masks will drop down from overhead. Put your mask on before you help your kids put theirs on."

It seems counterintuitive, but the reality is, you have to be breathing in order to help anyone else.

So, you have to look after you in order to be able to look after anyone else.

God is a God of unlimited capacity. We are all limited in some way in our capacity. God could do anything He wanted to do but is often limited to working in our lives—not because of His capacity but because of ours.

The limitation is not God. It's you. It's me.

God is always able. Exceedingly, abundantly above and beyond able. But I am limited. By my fears. My insecurities. My self-doubts. My limited thinking.

God is super abundant. He has created a world full of abundance. The real limitation, ultimately, is me.

So, you really are the most important person in your life.

45

An estimate is the lie you tell yourself to get started on a project.

Every project takes longer and costs more than you originally expect. It happens every time.

Knowing this can prevent us from a lot of disappointment. We just have to know there is no way we can anticipate every cost and every hurdle.

I remember when we built our first building for our church. I had never had to tackle a multi million dollar building project before. Much less, lead a church into helping make it happen.

There was no way I could know all the details and obstacles I would face.

But I grew into the project, and it set me up to now tackle more building projects.

Know it will cost more than you think. It will take longer than you imagine. But you will grow into it.

46

Goals are great because of the person you have to become to achieve them.

I've always been a goal-oriented type of person. I think my motivations for accomplishing those goals have changed over time.

At first, I thought accomplishing goals would make me a worthwhile person who could be admired by others. It took me a while to realize that people don't actually care that much whether I weigh 180 or 200 pounds.

The value of a goal to me now is—it shows me who I need to become, what I need to learn, and what adjustments I need to make in order to reach that goal.

So, I have health goals, financial goals, spiritual goals, work goals, all kinds of goals.

Sometimes (many times), I don't completely reach those goals. But I do become a better person as I make the adjustments necessary to try and reach those goals.

You don't have to reach every goal every time. But keep setting goals for the person it will help you become.

47

God is always, eventually faithful.

It's easy to make a judgement on things too soon.

When it feels like things are not going your way today, you have to stop, breathe, pray, and give it some time.

Having walked with God for almost fifty years now helps me have a long-term perspective.

God is at work, often doing more behind the scenes than you realize. He is faithful to His Word, faithful to His Promise.

I've often wanted things to happen that weren't happening the way I'd hoped. When I look back now, I'm glad they didn't happen the way I first imagined. God was faithful.

When you're having a season where it seems God isn't working, give it a minute. Remember His faithfulness in the past. You will have another story to tell of His faithfulness over this season too.

48

Lack of communication is the breeding ground for vain imaginations.

I can't even begin to count how many times I have thought someone was thinking or leaning in a certain direction and then later discovered I was all wrong.

It's amazing how we can create entire scenarios in our own head about what's going on in someone else's head.

I've found this to be true in my marriage, with my family, on my team, with friends, and even with some enemies.

So many times, when I have actually sat down with someone face to face, I have realized I made up in my own head what they were thinking.

Communication is actually hard, continuous work. Both parties have to want to lean into each other and make the effort to stay in touch and communicate.

Don't ever assume you know what someone else is thinking until you actually find out what they are thinking.

49

The God who created everything, owns everything, & controls everything is FOR you.

The God who is fully aware of all our imperfections and inconsistencies has chosen, out of His amazing love, to take a posture toward us—HE IS FOR US.

He could have chosen any posture He wanted. He's God; He sets the rules.

He chose this posture—I am for you!

Some people want to paint a picture of a God who is always on the verge of disappointment with us, ready to pour out some kind of judgment on any little slip up.

If God be for us, then who, or what, can be against us?

Unfortunately, not everyone is for you. Sometimes, we are not even for ourselves.

I often have to remind myself of this. God is always for me, no matter what is going on around me or even in me.

God is always for you and is always working things out for your good.

50

Build in the valley what God has shown you on the mountain.

Mountain top moments, mountain top visions are those special places or moments where we see the possibilities in their most vivid clarity.

The picture becomes clear. The revelation is unveiled. The potential is revealed.

You have to have that mountain top pattern to build by.

Then we have to walk down into the valley and start living and building out of what we saw on the mountain top.

The valley is where we walk it out; work it out.

The valley is not nearly as exciting as the mountain top.

The person who can actually build in the valley the vision they saw on the mountain is a gift to us all.

So keep walking, keep building, out of your mountain top vision, not out of your valley circumstances.

51

"Sorry" won't win the battle.

I was a young believer trying to get up in the morning and develop some kind of prayer life, and I had slept in— again.

In the shower, I was telling the Lord I was sorry—again.

As clear as a bell, the Holy Spirit spoke to my heart: "I love you, son, but sorry won't win the battle."

That phrase has lived in my heart for decades.

Prayer and prayer times do not earn us brownie points with God. There's nothing we can do—or not do—to make God love us more.

I was still on my way to Heaven. Still loved by God. But I was losing the battle.

There is a battle going on for all of us; for our calling, for our families, for the purposes of God in the earth.

If you're struggling to win the battle, let me encourage you. Keep getting up and trying. Again, and again.

52

You are not the star of the show.

If you want your life to count, you have to give your life to something bigger than you.

All of our lives are like a book or a movie—many scenes, many chapters.

God does want to bless your story, your movie. But He also wants us to realize we are not the real star of the show. He is!

I don't want this to sound like some kind of false humility of some kind, but this realization helped me a lot.

When you quit trying to be the star of the show, your show actually gets better.

And realize, you as co-star, with God as star, is way better than trying to accomplish things in your own ability.

Your best life will be found when you stop seeing yourself as the star of the story and start seeing Jesus as the star while you are the supporting cast.

When you or I are the star, the show, the story is pretty small.

When Jesus is the star, the show becomes so much greater and bigger.

53

The right direction is more important than perfection.

Living with a perfectionist can be exhausting. I know because I live with one—me!

A commitment to excellence is a good thing. A commitment to perfection is impossible. It keeps you constantly reaching for something that is unattainable.

It keeps you and everyone around you disappointed and discouraged.

As long as young, sixteen-year-old King Uzziah of Judah sought the Lord, God prospered him.

Uzziah continued to seek God.

God is never completely found.

He's too big to be nailed down.

It's the pursuit.

As long as He was in the pursuit of God,
God released favor, prosperity, and wisdom to him.

Out of his search for God
Came everything he needed.

No matter what the area is, seeking God, getting healthy, building your financial resources, improving your family life, no one gets it all perfect.

But keep taking steps in the right direction; it's good for your soul.

54

You hear the signals you are tuned in to.

Around all of us there are all kinds of signals going out.

TV signals, radio signals, streaming signals, XM, AM, FM, Spotify, Pandora, podcasts. The list can go on and on.

You could listen to country music, rock, opera, talk radio, 70s music, and on and on.

All of those signals are in the air. All you have to do is tune in to them. Decide what you want to listen to.

The Bible says the mindset on the Spirit is life and peace. (Romans 8:)

Jesus said, "Be careful how you listen." (Luke 8:18)

The signals are out there:
Abundance or lack
Opportunity or obstacles
Positive or negative
Generous or stingy
Love or hate
Confidence or fear
Spirit or flesh

Decide what station you want to listen to. It's your choice, and it makes a big difference.

55

Stay in your lane.

There is an ease and a grace for you there.

All of us are uniquely gifted with a grace from Heaven to enable us to accomplish our purpose on Earth.

When we watch someone operating in their gift and grace, it just seems easy. It just flows.

You are a unique blend of personality, character traits, experiences, gifts, talents, perspectives, and lessons from the Lord.

When we watched Michael Jordan play basketball, it was magic. When he tried his hand at playing baseball, it was tragic. He stepped out of his lane.

A fish can flow swimming but not flying
A squirrel can flow climbing but not swimming

Your journey is to discover your gift(s) that grace has given you.

Your calling and purpose are written into your soul. You are gifted for God's purpose for your life.

When you locate your gifts, when you locate your grace, you locate your calling in life.

56

You can run your life from your prayer closet.

Jesus said, "But you, when you pray, go into your inner room, and when you have shut your door, pray to your Father who is in secret, and your Father who sees in secret will repay you in the open." (Matthew 6:6)

You can run your life from your prayer closet.

We pray in secret;
Our heavenly Father repays in the open.

Every decision needs a couple of passes through your prayer closet.

Everything you're thinking about saying (or not saying) needs a couple of passes through your prayer closet
You can make your task list from your prayer closet.
Instead of being distracted by the thought of tasks while praying, just quickly jot them down and move on.

You can move things in life by dealing with the issue in the spirit realm first.

The value of handling all the stuff of life first in the place of prayer first is enormously helpful in living your best life.

57

Sometimes, the best call is to defer.

I am pretty competitive, and I like to win. But trying to win every battle is not really winning in the long run.

We live in an angry day. People are fighting over political candidates, racial issues, and even bathroom issues. You don't hear much about deferring to one another.

Abraham deferred to Lot (Gen.13) when their herdsman were fighting each other: "You go to the left, I'll go right – or you go right, I'll go left." There's no use in us living in this contentious place. It's not the way life is supposed to be lived.

Abraham's deferring was not weakness. He was taking charge of an unpleasant situation and had the courage to make the change.

He believed in God's abundance & generosity and knew no matter which way he went, there was enough blessing to go around for both him & Lot.

I think a little more courageous deferring might be good for us.

58

It all started in a garden.

A blessed life in a blessed place was God's original intention for all of us.

God created mankind with a first intention to bless Him.

Blessed is God's default setting.

God's normal is blessed;

Man messed it up.

Jesus restores what man messes up.

Redemption, restoration is the Bible story.

Why a garden?

The kingdom of God operates with agricultural principles.

There are so many of Jesus's teachings, stories, and parables that are agricultural. It's not just because He lived in an agricultural society.

We live in a technological era.
But ultimately, real life happens more agriculturally.

Technology is quick, cuts some corners, and instant.

Real life doesn't work that way.

There are:
Seasons	Soil matters
Seeds	Weeds
Sowing and reaping	Rain – from Heaven
Fruit	

God's original, and current, intention is to bless your garden.

59

When you move, God moves.

So, make a move and give Him something to bless.

Often, people are waiting for God to move when He is actually waiting for us to make a move.

We become by doing, not just by hearing. Just because we think we know about something doesn't mean it's become a reality in our lives.

We have to take what we know and put it into action. Take a step of some kind. Make some kind of a move.

The four lepers in the 2 Kings 7 said to each other, "Why sit we here until we die?" When they launched out, they discovered the blessing God had set up for them.

Instead of waiting for the stop sign to turn green, make a move that God can bless.

60

Pray the promise, not the problem.

Just about every prayer recorded in the Bible starts with recognizing the greatness and faithfulness of God.

Great, effective prayer starts with God, not with the problem.

It's better to look at the problem from the perspective of the greatness of God rather than looking at God from the greatness of your problem.

This approach is not ignoring our problems; it's just recognizing God is so much greater than our problem.

Search out a promise from God related to your need. Let the Holy Spirit make one or two of those promises come alive in your spirit.

Then declare God's promise over whatever your need is.

Keep that promise in your mind, in your heart, and in your mouth.

61

There is a battle at the gate of every new season or level of life.

There are days when you say NO to your past and YES to your future.

There are gates we pass through in life
that mark "before" and "after" in our life.

Whenever you try to embark on a new project or endeavor of almost any kind, there will be a battle at the gate of the new beginning.

Starting a new ministry, adding another service, a new building project—starting almost any personal project where you are trying to personally launch into a new level.

There is a battle for breakthrough at the gates of new seasons, **new levels.** When you step up to the gate of the next season, when you walk through the gates that previously stood as barriers, you experience breakthrough.

Your breakthrough at the gate is not just for you. It will have an impact on everyone else in your world.

So, determine to win the battle at the gate.

62

Many decisions are made emotionally, and then a rationale is built afterward to justify that decision.

I'm not an emotional person and consider myself relatively level-headed and rational.

But I know I have made a lot of decisions based on how I felt around a certain group of people; how they treated me or valued me.

I have watched this same thing play out so many times with church people.

There have been people who thought our church was the best thing since sliced bread in one season, then have something (or someone) hurt their feelings, and all of a sudden, a list of what's wrong with our church starts to appear.

Our church hadn't really changed all that much. But now that their feelings were hurt, they had to build a rationale for why they should be upset with us.

Not all emotions involved in a decision are bad, but it is important to recognize how important and powerful the role emotions can play in affecting our decisions.

63

Planted people prosper.

Psalms 92:12-13: "The righteous person will flourish like the palm tree, Planted in the house of the LORD, They will flourish in the courtyards of our God."

You can imagine (actually, you probably couldn't!) how many people have come through the life of our church in the last three decades or over the last forty-two years I've been in full-time ministry.

The thousands of people who have moved on and on and on has been astounding.

There's no question, seasons change, and God moves people on to new chapters, new places, and new assignments.

But my observation—and trying to be as fair and objective as possible—is that so many people struggle with putting their roots down and just getting planted in the House of God.

As soon as a season of testing of any kind comes, they bounce on to the next place. And then the next place. And then the next place.

On the other hand, I've seen a handful of people get planted, put roots down, and flourish and prosper.

We have trees in our yard that have grown to tremendous heights. That never would have happened if we had continually uprooted them and kept moving them to different places.

Get planted in God's House and put some roots down!

64

**We don't see the world as it is.
We see the world as we are.**

Three guys are looking at a wheat field:
The artist sees a painting.
The farmer sees the harvest of wheat.
The developer sees land that could be used for building.

We create our world based on how we see the world:

How we see God
How we see ourselves
How we see life should be

So, how you see:
Money
Relationships
Work
Leadership
Family
Church
All that eventually shapes your world.

We all see things from our perspective.

We all take the picture from our angle.

The lifelong journey is: We just want to make sure our perspective continually moves to line up with God's perspective.

65

Face the facts and declare the truth.

The facts are not always the truth.

There is a difference between running our lives by facts or by truth.

The facts are pieces of information that surround us, and they are always changing.

The truth is principle that endures, no matter what the facts of the circumstances.

The facts may be:
You lost your job.
Your best friend walked out on you.
You got a bad report from the doctor.
You're in a tough season.

The truth is:
God is good.
He is for you.
He heals.
He provides.
He can always cause things to work out for your good.

The facts may create a comma or a pause; but don't ever put a period where God has just put a comma.

Joshua faced the fact there was a wall around Jericho, that there were giants in the city, but he declared the truth that God had given him the city.

Abraham faced the fact he was an old man, and Sarah was old as well, and he declared God was able to give him a child in his old age.

David faced the fact Goliath was a giant
but declared the truth: "My God is greater than you!"

We don't ignore the facts.
We just know there is a greater truth.

66

Wherever you go, there you are.

If you like Double Stuff Oreos in Louisiana, you will like them in North Carolina. Believe me, I know!

If you are always late in Nebraska, you will always be late in Georgia.

Because wherever you go, there you are!

People take their good qualities with them. People take their weaknesses with them—wherever they go.

So, maybe the solution is not a new job or a new location or a new church. Maybe the solution might be the man in the mirror.

So, wherever you are:
Be a worshipper
Be happy
Be grateful
Believe in God
Believe in yourself
Make good choices
Enjoy your life!

Printed in the USA
CPSIA information can be obtained
at www.ICGtesting.com
LVHW010429110823
754891LV00005B/96

9 781662 879616